STANMORE
& HARROW WEALD
PAST & PRESENT

DON WALTER

SUTTON PUBLISHING

Sutton Publishing Limited
Phoenix Mill · Thrupp · Stroud
Gloucestershire · GL5 2BU

First published 2007

Copyright © Don Walter, 2007

Title page photograph: A hard climb up
Stanmore Hill, *c.* 1919. *(Author's
Collection)*

British Library Cataloguing in Publication Data
A catalogue record for this book is available from the
British Library.

ISBN 978-0-7509-4263-8

Typeset in 10.5/13.5 Photina.
Typesetting and origination by
Sutton Publishing Limited.
Printed and bound in England by
J.H. Haynes & Co. Ltd, Sparkford.

This one is for Gwen and Deryck

CONTENTS

In this eighteenth-century engraving, a family is seen visiting the pound where straying animals were secured until claimed. Although the picture is clearly identified as 'at Stanmore, Middlesex' the pound's exact location has never been established. (*Harrow Local History Collection*)

INTRODUCTION

Few areas of the busy London Borough of Harrow are today considered more 'desirable' by local estate agents than Stanmore. For confirmation, you need only look at the sheer number of local businesses handling property sales and, even more conclusively, at the vast sums such properties are now commanding. Indeed, on the basis of property prices, the Halifax Building Society (HBOS) recently rated Stanmore as the eighth dearest area in the whole of the country.

And what amazing properties so many of them are – with singularly grandiose designs that often smack more of some tele-land setting (Dallas, for example) than the Middlesex/Hertfordshire borders. The London *Evening Standard* certainly shares this view. 'A quick stroll round Stanmore', they wrote in a 2004 article, 'shows you that not all of London's money is on show in West One', adding rather sourly 'No wonder (Stanmore's) Jubilee Line is silver!'

Jubilee Line or no (and the area also has another station at Canons Park), Stanmore folk, like their opposite numbers in the American soaps, rarely seem to walk and the present-day pictures in this book were taken by the author at some risk from passing cars!

It is also a curious fact that the ostentation displayed in some parts of Stanmore is by no means a new phenomenon. As long ago as 1888, the artist William Morris, having won a commission to design tapestries for the recently built Stanmore Hall, described the area as being 'much beset with gentlemen's houses', adding – in much the same dismissive vein – that it was 'pretty, after a fashion'.

Morris may well have been right in labelling some of the newer residents nouveau riche but the district itself could hardly have had a longer or more interesting pedigree, possibly extending to Roman times. Although conclusive evidence has yet to be unearthed, many historians have long believed that the Roman town of Sulloniacae (known to have been about 12 miles from Londinium and 9 from Verulamium, now St Albans) was sited on Brockley Hill, part of the former Watling Street which runs straight as an arrow on Stanmore's eastern borders.

What is incontrovertible is that Stanmore was a community in its own right, and thus no mere appendage to Harrow, at the time of the Domesday Book, William the Conqueror's great record of the lands he had wrested from King Harold. As early as 1086 the district was already split into two manors, Stanmere and Stanmera, each of around 9½ hides (equivalent in total to some 1,100 acres). And, for centuries, local people clearly belonged to either Great or Little Stanmore, a division now largely forgotten by all but a few die-hard historians.

The name Stanmere – a conflation of the Old English 'stan' and 'mere' meaning a stony mere or pool – is, in fact, recorded even earlier in a document of AD 793 in which King Offa of Mercia and his sons grant ten 'mansiones' (holdings) as part of the foundation of St Albans Abbey. At the time of Domesday, however, it was held by King

William's half-brother. At the same time, one Roger de Rames held Stanmera, later Little Stanmore and, later still, Whitchurch.

Just as Domesday recorded the presence of a priest on Harrow Hill well before the 1094 consecration of St Mary's, so too does a priest appear among those living at Great Stanmore, though the precise location of his presumed church is not known.

The first Stanmore church of which we have any real knowledge dates from medieval times. Dedicated (like the Harrow Church) to St Mary, it stood close to the moated manor house in what is now Old Church Lane (hence, of course, the name). Following its closure in 1632, it seems to have been largely forgotten until late nineteenth-century railway work uncovered clearly identifiable remains.

Today Great Stanmore and Little Stanmore can each lay claim to a church of un-common interest. Great Stanmore could be said to have two as the present-day St John's, consecrated in July 1850, has in its grounds the ruins of its predecessor, whose consecration was performed by Archbishop Laud, Charles I's Archbishop of Canterbury, exactly 218 years earlier.

Between 1714 and 1716, Little Stanmore gained St Lawrence, Whitchurch, whose lavish interior still remains a monument to the baroque style that is thought to be unique in Britain. Its generous patron was James Brydges, first Duke of Chandos, who also built himself the vast mansion called Canons which, for all its magnificence, survived for little more than a quarter of a century. Its smaller replacement, however, continues as the North London Collegiate School.

At various periods, Stanmore could boast – as many of our illustrations reveal – such vast residences as Stanmore Hall, Stanmore Park, The Grove and Warren House. Another grand establishment, Bentley Priory, was even for a while a royal residence, being the last home of the Dowager Queen Adelaide, widow of William IV. Over the centuries, Bentley Priory has assumed many roles, becoming a hotel in 1885, when the ambitious entrepreneur Frederick Gordon created a railway from Harrow largely for his guests. Ironically, the hotel failed but the railway – as our pictures show – continued to carry passengers to and from Stanmore well into the middle of the twentieth century.

Neighbouring Harrow Weald was far slower to develop, being for most of its history what the *Victoria County History of Middlesex* aptly describes as 'a large forested area unfavourable to settlement'. However, the early nineteenth-century Enclosure Acts did release areas of pleasant woodland that were subsequently acquired by wealthy Londoners as country residences. Among them was the fashionable artist Frederick Goodall, for whom Norman Shaw built the still surviving Grim's Dyke. Today it is best remembered as the home of Sir William Gilbert, the writing half of the great Gilbert & Sullivan partnership.

By the early 1900s the district was sufficiently well known to attract the attention of Sir Arthur Conan Doyle who made it the setting of 'The Affair of the Three Gables', published as part of *The Case-book of Sherlock Holmes*. Considerable interest was also attached to the tiny cottages of The City (so-called) at Old Redding, one of the earliest examples of a philanthropic employer (brick-maker Charles Blackwell) building a group of dwellings for his workers. At various points Stanmore and Harrow Weald rub shoulders with Belmont and Edgware, two communities whose past is infinitely richer than their somewhat anonymous present suggests. For this reason, they have been given their own small sections in this book, contributing to a diversity of images which, it is hoped, will provide as many discoveries for its readers as it did for its author.

Don Walter, 2006

1

Old & New St John's

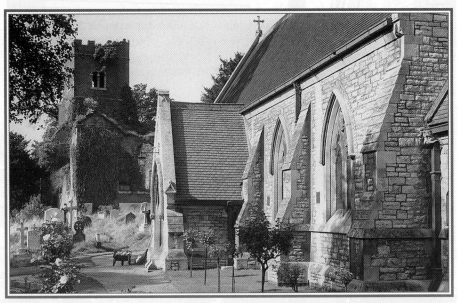

Given its prominent role in local history, any account of Great Stanmore must surely begin with the parish church of St John – or rather the two churches that still exist side by side on the same Church Road site. This picture shows the porch of the 'new' St John's with, in the background, the older, now ruined St John's as it looked for most of the last century, romantically covered in ivy. As a prelude to its total demolition, the roof and south wall were removed in 1850 but persistent agitation brought the destruction to a halt. The building still remains a noble structure which many consider should never have been allowed to fall into such disrepair that a new church was deemed necessary. *(Harrow Local History Collection)*

Stripped of the ivy that threatened to destroy it, the old St John's today reveals the red brick that was almost certainly made locally at the Harrow Weald kiln (see p. 108). Built at the personal expense of London merchant Sir John Wolstenholme, the church was consecrated in July 1632 by the then Bishop of London, William Laud. As Charles I's Archbishop of Canterbury, he was impeached and executed during the English Civil Wars. *(Author's Collection)*

This lithograph, made in about 1840 by the Bushey-based artist J.C. Oldmeadow, shows that the first St John's had an exceptionally handsome interior with many fine monuments that were later removed to the 'new' church. A 1990s 'consolidation' programme has ensured the long-term safety of the old building, enabling it to be opened regularly for guided tours. *(Harrow Local History Collection)*

The Borough of Harrow's only royal resident, the Dowager Queen Adelaide moved to the area following the death of her husband, William IV. From her home at Bentley Priory (see p. 49) she travelled regularly to St John's for Sunday worship, invariably choosing a rear pew so that the cough which ultimately contributed to her death would not disturb the congregation. Such consideration won her great respect and affection in the district. *(Author's Collection)*

Queen Adelaide made her last public appearance on 14 March 1849 at the ceremony at which the foundation stone was laid for the 'new' St John's. So large a crowd attended the occasion that, as this lively Oldmeadow lithograph shows, many were obliged to stand on tombs in the existing churchyard to ensure a view of the event. *(Author's Collection)*

The site for the second St John's was given by Lieutenant-Colonel Hamilton Tovey-Tennant whose splendid home, Pynnacles, can be glimpsed in the picture above of the foundation ceremony. Its name is now recalled by Pynnacles Close, a small street with very twenty-first-century flats just off Church Road. The original Pynnacles burnt down in 1930. *(Author's Collection)*

Built of Kentish rag and Bath stone in the Early Decorated Gothic style typical of its date, the second St John's is seen here in a photograph taken in about 1938 from the opposite side of Church Road. The Rector, the Revd Douglas Gordon, gave £1,000 towards its cost and his father (Lord Aberdeen) some £5,000, while £3,000 came from a general rate imposed on the parishioners. *(Harrow Local History Collection)*

Virtually the same view from 2005 shows remarkably little change apart from the acquisition of a well-trimmed hedge – and a bus shelter! The wooden lychgate was given by Sir John Kelk in memory of his sons. For about 30 years until 1881, Kelk was the owner of Bentley Priory. *(Author's Collection)*

This delightfully animated mid-nineteenth-century print shows St John's (flying an improbably large flag) with its adjoining rectory. History records that the latter was not built until almost 100 years after the 1632 consecration and then only at the personal expense of the rector of the day, Dr George Hudson. Timbers used in its construction were said to have been given by the Duke of Chandos (see p. 93). *(Harrow Local History Collection)*

Though photographs of the old rectory taken in the 1950s show a building that had apparently survived with its period charms intact, it was found necessary to demolish it in 1960. It was then replaced by this modern and undoubtedly more convenient house. *(Author's Collection)*

The Victorian ambience of today's St John's is greatly heightened by the picturesque Hollond Lodge on the fringe of the churchyard. Designed by the architect Brightwen Binyon, who did considerable work in Stanmore, it was erected in 1881. It commemorates local benefactor Robert Hollond who, in his younger days, famously travelled in a hot-air balloon from London's Vauxhall Gardens to the Netherlands. (*Author's Collection*)

The small green that today adjoins St John's now houses its own little piece of history – the bowl of what was once a drinking fountain (see p. 35) given to the village by Agnes Keyser of Warren House, a platonic friend of King Edward VII in whose name she founded the now famous hospital 'for officers' in London. (*Author's Collection*)

Great Stanmore's ecclesiastical history is even richer than the foregoing pictures suggest for there is evidence of both a Saxon church and a medieval church on the same site in the now aptly named Old Church Lane. The foundations of this latter building were uncovered in about 1890 during excavations for the proposed Stanmore-Harrow railway (see p. 41). *(Harrow Local History Collection)*

From these discoveries contemporary historian and archaeologist Hugh Braun was able to construct this diagram showing the probable floor plan of the medieval church. In common with the surviving church on nearby Harrow Hill, consecrated in 1094, the Stanmore church was dedicated to St Mary. The railway excavations also uncovered many graves of which the only survivor is that of the Revd Baptist Willoughby, appointed rector in 1563. *(Harrow Local History Collection)*

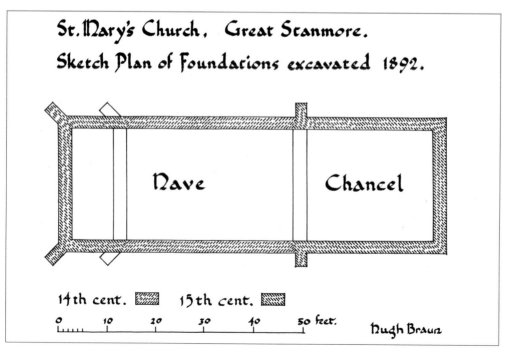

St. Mary's Church, Great Stanmore.
Sketch Plan of Foundations excavated 1892.

Nave   Chancel

14th cent.   15th cent.

0   10   20   30   40   50 feet.

Hugh Braun

By the time this picture was taken in the first decades of the twentieth century the Manor House that had once adjoined the medieval church in Old Church Lane had acquired a stucco-covered brick façade which effectively disguised its sixteenth-century origins. The property was demolished in 1930. *(Harrow Local History Collection)*

In complete contrast, the still-surviving New Manor House further along Old Church Lane looks far older than it actually is, having been built as The Crofts in 1901. Thirty years later it was remodelled for Samuel Wallrock on the pseudo-Tudor lines shown in this picture of 1933. *(Harrow Local History Collection)*

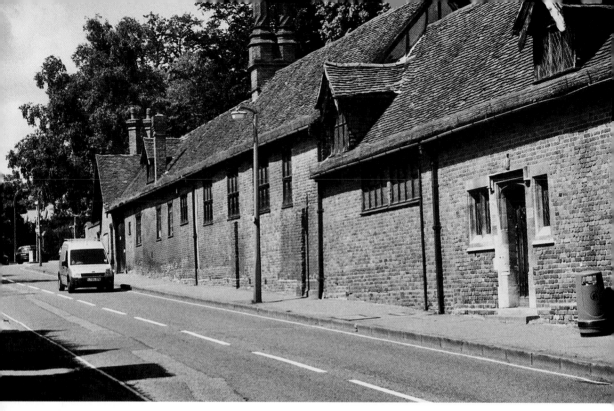

When Wallrock went bankrupt in 1932, St John's Church took over this interesting group of buildings at the Church Road end of Old Church Lane. Originally outbuildings on the Wallrock estate, they currently serve as a church hall and verger's house. In recent years the New Manor House itself has been maintained by the Ministry of Defence as a residence for the Air Commodore at Bentley Priory. *(Author's Collection)*

A further reminder of Wallrock's taste for all things Tudor is the well-head that once graced his grounds, now found at the entrance to a cul-de-sac of relatively modern homes near the St John's end of Old Church Lane. The road's name is not surprising. *(Author's Collection)*

2

Stanmore Broadway & Church Road

Although this early twentieth-century postcard identifies itself as London Road, this particular stretch of today's busy A410 is now known as Stanmore Broadway. The horse and cart, having just passed Pathgate (now Cottrell) Cottages, is heading for today's Church Road and is about to pass the village pond dug in about 1640 where collected surface water was supplemented by water piped down from the Spring Ponds (see p. 83). *(Author's Collection)*

By the First World War the first commercial developments (right) were already beginning to transform the sleepy centre of the village into today's thronged Broadway. However, as the prolific greenery on the left of the picture suggests, the far side of the road was then in residential use. *(Author's Collection)*

Opposite, top: In this later, wider view of The Broadway, the eighteenth-century Buckingham Cottage on the opposite corner is revealed in all its picturesque charm. But there are already twin islands opposite its front door, providing a hint of the traffic problems soon to come. *(Author's Collection)*

Opposite, bottom: In October 1961 Buckingham Cottage fell beneath the demolitionists' hammer and a parade of shops arose in its place, seen here in 1970. The developers forged a somewhat fragile link with the past by calling it Buckingham Parade; nevertheless to many its destruction signalled the end of Stanmore as a village. *(Harrow Local History Collection)*

In 1980 the area underwent another major change with the construction of a massive block named Fanum House as headquarters for the Automobile Association. Its uncompromisingly eighties styling provided a curious contrast with the 1870s mock-Gothic of its immediate neighbour, the Bernays Institute (far right). *(Harrow Local History Collection)*

Opposite, top: In 2006 the Bernays Institute looks very different from its neighbours, being sandwiched between the one-time AA building, now housing a vast carpet showroom, and a highly contemporary Sainsbury's superstore. Built in 1870, the Institute commemorates Ernest Bernays, the son of Stanmore's then rector, who was drowned while swimming in the river at Glengariff, Ireland. *(Author's Collection)*

Opposite, bottom: For nearly 60 years, the Bernays family have also been recalled by a small but delightful public open space known as the Bernays Gardens, with its entry in Church Road. The three-quarter-acre site was once part of Samuel Wallrock's estate and is still bordered by some of the original outbuildings to which he added quasi-Tudor embellishments. *(Author's Collection)*

One of Stanmore's most interesting buildings, the former Pathgate or Broadway Cottages, was probably built as a single house for the Burnell family in the seventeenth century. A jettied timber-framed construction, it lost its westernmost bay to demolition in 1865; nevertheless it remains an impressive 98ft long. *(Harrow Local History Collection)*

Handsomely restored by a Mr Cottrell in 1968 (when it was renamed Cottrell Cottages), the building is now primarily used for offices. Earlier uses have included a coal business with stables at the rear, the home of the district nurse and midwife and, earlier still, many years as a farmhouse. *(Author's Collection)*

Short in length – it runs only from Green Lane to Stanmore Hill – Church Road is long in history and, a century ago, had many interesting buildings, among them The Fountain public house (right). In the adjoining ivy-clad cottages Stanmore's first telephone exchange was installed in 1905. The pub may not always have been as peaceful as our picture suggests for, in the 1870s, its proprietor was instructed 'to conduct his house in a more respectable manner'. *(Harrow Local History Collection)*

In this further view of early twentieth-century Church Road, Bedford Stores (with canopy) is seen on the left adjoining the telephone exchange. The curious object on the right, on which a small boy is precariously perched, has been variously described as a water container and a water pump. *(Author's Collection)*

Known as Elm Terrace, these small wooden buildings were also a feature of turn-of-the-twentieth-century Church Road close to the present Elm Park Road. Nearby a specially gravelled space was reserved for the carriages of the gentry attending service at St John's while their horses were given stabling at the Crown. *(Harrow Local History Collection)*

Church Road today, seen from the junction with Elm Park Road, is your typical contemporary High Street, housing both familiar retail names and more specialised local shops including a 'boulangerie'. Once this part of the village had grown, it became the site for a replacement for Stanmore's original post office, first opened on Stanmore Hill in 1893. *(Author's Collection)*

In an undated but probably 1920s photograph, Church Road is shown from outside its oldest public house. Called the Crown, it was once owned by Stanmore's very own brewers, the Clutterbucks (see p. 32), and licensed as early as 1803. *(Author's Collection)*

In 2006 the Crown lives on but with a new frontage and the kind of new name – the Crazy Horse – deemed to be of appeal to a younger generation of drinkers. As its signage proudly proclaims, it is also 'a gourmet burger bar'. *(Author's Collection)*

In this charming watercolour of 1880 by Edward Arthur Phipson, the north side of Church Road, opposite Elm Park Road, still retains the picturesque look of a village street. The house on the right is even older than it appears here, being a timber-framed building thought to date from 1680 with eighteenth-century additions. *(Author's Collection)*

Though considerably altered – and somewhat overshadowed by the adjoining restaurant (left) – today's 21 Church Road is, in fact, the building shown to the right of the watercolour above. Currently occupied by a construction company, it now bears the name of Regent House, recalling the Prince Regent's visit to Stanmore in 1814 (see p. 37). *(Author's Collection)*

In 1920 two little girls amble along Elm Park Road, off Church Road, then described as 'a wide road of gravel and grass with dog roses growing down each side'. Fifty years later, when this picture was reproduced in the local press, one of the girls identified herself to the editor, commenting how sorry she was 'to see the old Stanmore go'. *(Author's Collection)*

Elm Park Road today houses many significant buildings, including Stanmore College and, at the Church Road end, this vehicle and pedestrian entry to a Sainsbury's supermarket. Fortunately for residents, a gate, glimpsed here in the middle distance, offers some protection from the traffic. *(Author's Collection)*

Photographed between the two world wars, Glebe Road (off The Broadway) has strong ecclesiastical connections, having once been glebe land set aside for the upkeep of the parish priest. *(Author's Collection)*

In the 80 years or so since the picture above was taken, Glebe Road has gained a few more houses but has lost little of its peacefulness, especially when contrasted with the clamour of The Broadway only yards away. Part of the road, once earmarked for a church hall, had to be deconsecrated before private developers could build. *(Author's Collection)*

3

Stanmore Hill

Climbing steeply out of the old village to the Middlesex–Hertfordshire border, Stanmore Hill remains one of the district's most distinctive roads despite the loss of many interesting buildings, such as these old cottages at the very foot of the hill. The one on the left originally housed the Queen's Head public house, site of many a vestry meeting before it was moved across the road. This picture was taken in about 1870, making it possibly the oldest in this book. *(Harrow Local History Collection)*

By the 1890s the property shown on p. 29 had become the butcher's shop of A.S. Ginger. In a world without petrol fumes or rigid health and hygiene regulations, Mr Ginger – and presumably his customers – was entirely happy for his choicest meat to be displayed uncovered and virtually in the road. As in the picture on p. 29, there is a clockmaker on the right, almost certainly the business run by R. Leversutch. *(Harrow Local History Collection)*

Like so many surviving photographs, this view of a peaceful Stanmore Hill is taken from a postcard. Its postmark gives a date of August 1902, by which time the Queen's Head had moved to its new location (left). Its neighbours included a picturesque mix of small cottages and larger residential properties, including a house with a highly distinctive bay window at first floor level (middle distance). *(Harrow Local History Collection)*

A decade or so later, the same properties remain but the hill has now acquired its first telegraph poles as well as an open-topped bus on the 142 route to and from Watford. Obviously a much-welcomed addition to local transport, vehicles on this route feature in a great many pictures of the period. *(Harrow Local History Collection)*

In 2006 the camera's view of the present buildings at the foot of Stanmore Hill is all but obscured by constantly flowing traffic. The not unattractive red-brick structure on the far right is Stanmore's much-patronised public library. *(Author's Collection)*

Stanmore once laid claim not only to a goodly number of inns but also to its very own brewery. Called Clutterbucks after its mid-eighteenth-century founder, Thomas Clutterbuck, it operated from notably attractive buildings at the very top of Stanmore Hill, including the block with cupola and clocktower (left) used as the original brew-house. It is shown here nearly 30 years ago when it housed Pattissons, manufacturer of golf course maintenance equipment. (*Harrow Local History Collection*)

When the old brewery was featured in the local paper, the *Harrow Observer*, in 1978, most of its buildings still survived, including this cobbled stableyard. Clutterbucks had eight 'tied' houses in Stanmore alone and more than 70 elsewhere. For a time, the brewery even grew its own hops in a field on the Warren House estate (see p. 63) while essential water was drawn from an artificial pond across the road known as Brewers' Pond. (*Harrow Local History Collection*)

In January 1906 workers from Clutterbucks turn out in one of the brewery's drays in support of the local Liberal Unionist candidate, the Hon. W.H. Peel. The picture was taken outside the Masons Arms on the corner of Edgware High Street and Whitchurch Lane. *(Harrow Local History Collection)*

As seen in this contemporary view, much of the original brewery has survived, including the clocktower, though the buildings' use is now wholly residential. Sadly, the Clutterbuck name (which provided Stanmore with its last Lord of the Manor) has been banished – to be replaced by the grand but somewhat meaningless Lancaster House, Park Lane. *(Author's Collection)*

This 1919 souvenir of the top of Stanmore Hill recalls the final days of Clutterbucks with the brewery itself, then owned by the Cannon Brewery, in the far distance (left) and one of its earliest houses, the Vine, on the right. At the time of the photograph, the 142 bus service was only some six years old. *(Author's Collection)*

Eighty-seven years later, the 142 service is still routed via the Vine, whose external appearance has changed remarkably little. The passengers boarding in this May 2006 photograph are, however, wearing Middle Eastern dress, serving as a reminder of recent changes in the ethnic base of Stanmore's population. *(Author's Collection)*

Stanmore Hill, at its junction with Green Lane, is here pictured in Edwardian days when its most prominent feature was a combined street lamp and fountain-cum-water trough given to the village by local noteworthy, Agnes Keyser of Warren House (see p. 63). Just visible beyond the horse and cart is the entrance to the historic Abercorn Arms. *(Author's Collection)*

The water fountain was still in place when this further view was taken some time during the First World War. The soldier and sailor (far left) have since been identified as C. Holland and A. Brinkman. Note, too, the advertisements for the increasingly popular motoring products on the white clapboard premises in the background. *(Harrow Local History Collection)*

The white clapboard building happily remains today although lamp and fountain have long since vanished from the scene. The fountain's bowl, however, has survived and, as recorded on p. 13, can now be found outside St John's Church in Church Road. *(Author's Collection)*

The nineteenth-century Stanmore Hill could boast not one but two schools – an Infants' School built in 1845 and, subsequently, this so-called National School opened in 1861 south of the earlier school. The latter, shown here in the 1920s, was demolished in 1971. *(Harrow Local History Collection)*

In this mid-nineteenth-century engraving, the Watford coach is seen arriving at the Abercorn Arms. The 'Royal' inscription on the wall behind the coach refers to the momentous meeting there in 1814 between the Prince Regent (later George IV) and Louis XVIII of France, when they discussed the future of the defeated Napoleon Bonaparte. *(Harrow Local History Collection)*

Some 100 years later, long-distance patrons of the Abercorn were more likely to arrive on the Watford–Stanmore bus. Always a prominent player on the Stanmore scene, the Abercorn was occasionally used as a local courthouse and vestry meeting place. In 1820 its proprietor John Seabrook became the village's first postmaster. *(Author's Collection)*

Spruce and welcoming, the Stanmore Hill house remains a popular hostelry. Though still proudly known as 'the Abercorn' the inn-sign no longer shows the heraldic arms of the Abercorn family who had been in residence at Bentley Priory since 1790. (*Author's Collection*)

Now under the proprietorship of Ember Inns, the Abercorn's sign currently features a fire with glowing embers rather than the original coat of arms of the Abercorn family. Something of a pillar of society, the first Marquess numbered among his guests at Bentley Priory political figures such as the Duke of Wellington and the writers Walter Scott and William Wordsworth. (*Author's Collection*)

Having been granted Post Town status in 1829, Stanmore acquired its first purpose-built post office on Stanmore Hill in 1893. The postmaster was then Thomas Berwick who, like his father before him, combined his postal work with a successful business as a grocer and wine merchant in the adjoining premises. *(Author's Collection)*

In 2006 a firm of chartered surveyors and a hairdressing salon occupy the old post office and adjoining grocers. Possibly because of the extreme steepness of the Hill, the postal business moved from this site in 1932 into new and undoubtedly more convenient premises down the Hill in Church Road. *(Author's Collection)*

Today it is worth the steep walk up and down the Hill to see other fine residences, notably the Georgian building at no. 73, variously known as Loscombe Lodge and Robin Hill. It was for a while the lodgings of Dr Edmund Wilson who, in 1912, died a hero's death with Captain Scott on the latter's ill-fated Antarctic expedition. *(Author's Collection)*

Also still standing, if much changed, is the aptly titled Hill House. Now transformed into apartments, it has been home to both the eighteenth-century scholar Samuel Parr and the antiquarian Charles Fortnum of Fortnum & Mason fame. Parr, who had been Sheridan's tutor at Harrow School, actually opened his own school in Hill House in 1771 but the venture was short-lived. *(Author's Collection)*

4

The Harrow–Stanmore Railway

For all that the district can currently lay claim to two railway stations, Stanmore in London Road and Canons Park in Whitchurch Lane, the station and line most fondly remembered by older residents has now been closed for some 40 years. Little more than 2 miles in length, this was the branch line running from Harrow & Wealdstone station to a newly built Stanmore station in today's Gordon Road. It is shown here in 1969, a few years after its closure and one year before its demolition. *(Author's Collection)*

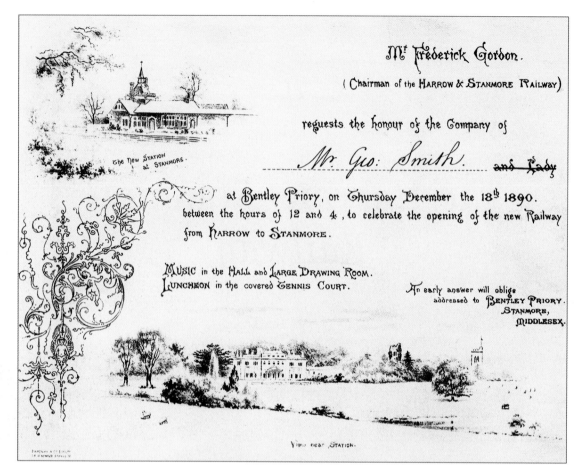

Mr Frederick Gordon.

(Chairman of the HARROW & STANMORE RAILWAY)

requests the honour of the Company of

Mr Geo. Smith and Lady

at Bentley Priory, on Thursday December the 18th 1890. between the hours of 12 and 4, to celebrate the opening of the new Railway from HARROW to STANMORE.

MUSIC in the HALL and LARGE DRAWING ROOM.
LUNCHEON in the covered TENNIS COURT.

An early answer will oblige
addressed to BENTLEY PRIORY.
STANMORE,
MIDDLESEX.

The New Station at STANMORE.

View near STATION.

As can be seen from this picture taken from an early but undated postcard, Stanmore's new acquisition was the very epitome of an English country station of the late Victorian era, complete with hanging flower baskets and advertisements for some of the leading suppliers of the day. As such, it was later to exercise great appeal for film and TV programme makers. *(Harrow Local History Collection)*

Opposite, top: The Stanmore branch line was largely the brainchild of the London hotelier Frederick Gordon who, having purchased the vast Bentley Priory in 1881 for use as a hotel, sought a reliable means of transporting guests literally to its door. As this invitation to the opening day's events reveals, it was December 1890 before his ambitious scheme was completed. *(Author's Collection)*

Opposite, bottom: To their credit the Great Stanmore Parish Council of the day insisted that the new station be at least as picturesque as the rest of the village. In response, Gordon and his partners, the London & North Western Railway, produced this small but charmingly decorated structure with a distinctly ecclesiastical look. *(Harrow Local History Collection)*

Although Gordon's hotel venture was sadly short-lived, his railway line continued as a much appreciated feature of local life until 1952 when it was closed to passengers. Inevitably, there was no lack of local photographers to record the various stages of the station's demise, such as this late 1960s shot showing the main station entrance stripped of its roof tiles. *(Harrow Local History Collection)*

By 2006 the old station house had been a private residence for over three decades. The road in which it stands is now called Gordon Avenue in honour of the hotelier who, following his death in Monte Carlo, was brought home for burial in the Stanmore church of St John's. *(Author's Collection)*

In this evocative glimpse of Gordon Avenue in about 1912, two ladies are safely strolling down the middle of the roadway where the only visible traffic is a slowly departing horse and cart. On their left is Cheyne Cottage overlooking the golf course. The latter was also created by Frederick Gordon in the hope of attracting well-heeled families to the area. *(Harrow Local History Collection)*

Cheyne Cottage remains one of Gordon Avenue's most attractive properties. Its somewhat unexpected bell-tower (also glimpsed in the earlier picture) was apparently designed as a kind of dinner-gong to summon golfers playing on the adjoining links! *(Author's Collection)*

This illustration of Evian House at 7 Gordon Avenue, first seen in *The Builder* of March 1892, shows exactly the kind of handsome house Frederick Gordon wanted to see in Stanmore. According to the same magazine, it was one of five properties 'of varying dimensions' that had already been built in the road. *(Harrow Local History Collection)*

Gordon Avenue today still has its share of attractive and substantial family homes. Other sites, like the present (and clearly identified) no. 7, have become apartment blocks, albeit of the most resplendent kind. *(Author's Collection)*

Originally known simply as Stanmore, Gordon's little station later had its name changed to Stanmore Village to avoid confusion after this modest terminus was built in London Road as part of a Metropolitan Line extension from Wembley Park. *(Harrow Local History Collection)*

Today's Stanmore station in London Road is still the end of the line for countless commuters. The line, however, is now the Jubilee, whose trademark colour of silver is seen – at least by cynical outsiders – as highly appropriate to the area! *(Author's Collection)*

5

Bentley Priory

Augustinian priory, royal residence, de-luxe hotel, girls' school, Battle of Britain Headquarters; Bentley Priory has been all of these in an exciting history unequalled by any other mansion in the borough or, for that matter, the county. Rarely out of the news, it was again hitting the headlines as this book was being written, following reports of the likely departure of its present occupiers, the Royal Air Force, and a subsequent sale for private development. *(Author's Collection)*

Originally a thirteenth-century priory of Augustinian canons, Bentley Priory first came to prominence as a home when in about 1788 the first Marquess of Abercorn employed the celebrated architect Sir John Soane to make major alterations to an earlier house. By 1848, when this view appeared in the *Illustrated London News*, it was the home of Queen Adelaide (queen dowager and widow of King William IV) where, failing in health, she was visited by Queen Victoria and Prince Albert. *(Harrow Local History Collection)*

By August 1885, when this advertisement was printed in *Punch*, Queen Adelaide had been dead some 36 years and the property had been acquired as a hotel by the entrepreneur Frederick Gordon. As recorded on p. 42, Gordon spent a fortune in bringing a railway line virtually to the hotel's door. *(Harrow Local History Collection)*

Like other vast mansions in the locality, Bentley Priory later became a school – a very superior school for young ladies which flourished from 1908 to the early 1920s. Here one of its great rooms has been transformed into an art studio. *(Author's Collection)*

Though taking its name from the thirteenth-century priory, the present mansion does not necessarily stand on the actual site of the original foundation, which passed into secular hands in 1546. Expert opinion believes that Priory House, the former Priory Farm on the southern edge of Bentley Park, is a more likely location. Priory House, which has been considerably rebuilt over the centuries, is seen here in a mid-1930s photograph. *(Harrow Local History Collection)*

To older generations at least Bentley Priory is best known for the years from 1925 when it was first acquired by the Air Ministry, becoming the Headquarters of Fighter Command 11 years later. As this picture of the now-celebrated Second World War Operations Room recalls, it was from here that Air Chief Marshal Sir Hugh Dowding directed the country's air defences during the Battle of Britain. When subsequently honoured, it was entirely appropriate that he should take the title Baron Dowding of Bentley Priory. *(Author's Collection)*

In autumn 2005, the Common Road entrance to the estate is still clearly identified as 'Royal Air Force – Bentley Priory': but for how much longer? An official spokesman has promised that 'the RAF will work closely with Defence Estates, English Heritage and the council with the intention of maintaining [its] proud history and unique part in this nation's history'. *(Author's Collection)*

As befits a great estate, entry to Bentley Priory was guarded by a number of lodges of which the most interesting survivor can be seen where Uxbridge Road meets the appropriately named Old Lodge Way. In addition to its attractively carved barge-boarding, the lodge's façade still boasts a feature that even the Abercorn Arms (see p. 38) lacks – the coat of arms of the Abercorn family. *(Author's Collection)*

6

More Great Houses

A hundred years ago, Bentley Priory was but one of a number of truly grand mansions in the district. Most have long since disappeared or been totally transformed for twenty-first-century living. The Grove, whose conservatory (seen above) once rivalled those at Kew, remains only as a street name but, for 34 years from 1872, it was the home of the celebrated naturalist and writer, Eliza Brightwen, who filled it with botanical rarities from all over the world. *(Harrow Local History Collection)*

Although The Grove was first recorded as early as 1788, the house seen here had been extensively remodelled for the Brightwens in the late 1870s. Its setting, Warren Lane, was even more historic, having been in medieval times part of an extensive coney warren belonging to the Lord of the Manor. (*Harrow Local History Collection*)

In old age Eliza Brightwen is seen serenely contemplating the garden idyll she had created all around her. After her death in 1906 – and her burial in the churchyard of St John's – her home was purchased by Sir Edward Cassel as a gift for his daughter Edwina, later Lady Mountbatten. (*Harrow Local History Collection*)

A family group, showing Mrs Brightwen with her nephew, the poet Edmund Gosse and his children, also recalls The Grove's golden years which ended with demolition in 1979. (*Harrow Local History Collection*)

Lower Grove Farm, however, lives on. Once part of the considerable Grove Estate, it is probably now best known as a riding school. An extensive survey of Harrow's old hedgerows, carried out at the end of the twentieth century, suggested that some of the farm's hedges date from late Tudor or early Stuart times. (*Author's Collection*)

Of the many mansions that positively flaunted the wealth of their Victorian owners, Stanmore Hall in Wood Lane is the only one to survive with much of its early grandeur intact. Originally built in 1843 and occupied by the notable balloonist Robert Hollond (see p. 13), it was virtually rebuilt half a century later as a kind of Gothic castle for William Knox D'Arcy, an entrepreneur who had literally struck gold (in Queensland) and oil (in Persia). *(Author's Collection)*

Opposite: In acknowledgement of Knox D'Arcy's desire to live in a castle, architect Brightwen Binyon added an impressive turret staircase, as shown in this evocative drawing dated May 1897, which subsequently appeared in *Building News*. Knox D'Arcy also employed William Morris for much of the Hall's interior decoration, including a series of tapestries on which Morris worked with the equally celebrated Edward Burne-Jones. *(Author's Collection)*

Turret · Staircase ·
STANMORE · HALL

Brightwen Binyon
Archt del
Ipswich
Mar 92.

Stanmore Hall's future seemed far from secure in 1977 when the house was extensively damaged by fire. By then, it had long ceased to be a private residence, becoming a wartime officers' mess for the nearby RAF and subsequently a nurses' home for the Royal National Orthopaedic Hospital. *(Harrow Local History Collection)*

Now restored to residential use, Stanmore Hall today houses what are reputedly among Stanmore's – and, quite possibly, Britain's – most expensive apartments. According to the national press, film stars Nicole Kidman, Tom Cruise and Leonardo di Caprio all expressed their interest. Some local residents, however, were less enthusiastic, complaining that the new wing (left) spoiled the view of the original roofline as seen from Little Common. *(Author's Collection)*

Long before it gave its name to an RAF station, Stanmore Park was another of Stanmore's great estates. At its heart was the house, seen here in an 1815 engraving, that was originally home to Andrew Drummond. A man of humble origins, Drummond rose in the early eighteenth century to become founder of Drummond's Bank at Charing Cross. His bank was subsequently absorbed into the Royal Bank of Scotland. *(Harrow Local History Collection)*

Like many grand houses too vast for single family occupancy, Stanmore Park became a boys' preparatory school in the late 1880s when many of its beautifully proportioned rooms were transformed into classrooms. The school's popularity was greatly enhanced by the appointment as headmaster of the Lancashire and England cricketer, the Revd Vernon Fanshawe Royle. In 1937 it moved from Stanmore to Hertfordshire. *(Author's Collection)*

As shown in this aerial view of 1932, Warren House in Wood Lane impressed by both its scale and its setting. From 1813 it was the home of Sir Robert Smirke, architect of the British Museum, who apparently first dreamed of owning his own country retreat while working on additions to nearby Bentley Priory. Early in the twentieth century the house was occupied by international financier Henry Bischoffsheim. *(Harrow Local History Collection)*

Opposite, top: In April 1938 with the Second World War looming, the Stanmore Park estate was acquired by the Air Ministry as one of four operational centres for London's barrage balloon defences. To general horror, the historic house was demolished the following month. The site then became the RAF station shown opposite until its closure in 1997. *(Harrow Local History Collection)*

Opposite, bottom: Stanmore Park subsequently disappeared under a mountain of brick and concrete to become the single biggest housing project ever undertaken within the Borough of Harrow. Its 400-plus new houses and flats, including a high percentage of affordable housing, prompted outcries of 'homes for votes'. The only link with its notable past is provided by names such as Lady Aylesford Drive, which commemorates a previous resident. *(Author's Collection)*

King Edward VII arrives by car (centre) in June 1907 for a visit to the Bischoffsheims at Warren House. History records that the real attraction for the amorous monarch was the presence of fellow guest Alice Keppel, an ancestor of the Duchess of Cornwall. According to the local press, it was midnight before the royal visitor departed. *(Author's Collection)*

Although over 100 acres of its estate was acquired for Green Belt usage about 65 years ago, Warren House itself still stands. When money from the South African Gift to Britain Fund was subsequently used to transform it into a rest home, it was briefly rechristened Springbok House. Today, with its old name restored, it houses the Husaini Shia Islamic Centre. *(Author's Collection)*

7

Pubs with a Past

Given the convenience of their location on important through routes from London and Middlesex to Hertfordshire and beyond, Harrow Weald, Stanmore and especially Edgware have never lacked for hostelries. Many have inevitably been lost but a gratifying number remain, including the Seven Balls in Kenton Lane. In this brochure advertisement of 1905 it was already weathering the changes of a new century by offering not only 'good stabling' for the horse-borne traffic but 'a motor and cycle garage' for a slowly increasing number of two- and four-wheeled customers. *(Harrow Local History Collection)*

Early motor buses line up outside the Seven Balls in Kenton Lane in this highly evocative picture from 1912. Although the service to and from Charing Cross originally ran only on Sundays and at Easter, residents subsequently complained with such vigour about the noise of the solid-tyre buses that the service was withdrawn! *(Harrow Local History Collection)*

As part of its 1993 refurbishment the Seven Bells ran a competition for a new swing sign, won by a local resident with a design featuring seven decorative orbs. The previous sign had depicted a game of bowls – although the inn's name is said to have been inspired by the coronet of the Duke of Chandos, allegedly decorated with seven golden balls. *(Author's Collection)*

Middlesex can only just lay claim to the Alpine, for its location in Common Road is within yards of the Hertfordshire border. The house has now been caring for travellers for well over 100 years, including a period in the 1880s (pictured) when it was known as the Alpine Coffee Tavern. As such, it was a mecca for the then fast developing bicycle clubs. *(Author's Collection)*

According to its present proprietors, who run it as a stylish restaurant, the Alpine still has its share of customers on two wheels. But now they must brave the heavy traffic which constantly passes its door in a world far removed from the one that once offered a meal of 'soup, cut from the joint, two veg, sweet and bread' for about half a crown. *(Author's Collection)*

Conveniently situated at the top of Brookshill where Old Redding meets Common Road, the Hare, seen here in Edwardian days, is the second pub in the area to bear this name. The first, licensed in 1702, stood on nearby Clamp Hill very much at the heart of the local brick-making industry. *(Author's Collection)*

Like the Red Lion (see p. 114) at Harrow Weald, the Hare has long had what is believed to be a sarsen stone on its forecourt to which later generations added a pump and drinking trough. All three features were still in place just before the Second World War when our photograph was taken. *(Harrow Local History Collection)*

Once owned by Stanmore's very own brewers, the Clutterbucks, the Hare is now part of a popular chain of restaurants-cum-pubs that focus as much attention on food as on drink. In external appearance, however, the building itself has changed remarkably little in a century, although forecourt pump and trough are long since gone. *(Author's Collection)*

Anyone taking the trouble to look today will still see the sarsen stone although, from time to time, it is apt to be overgrown by the surrounding greenery. Curiously enough, when our picture was taken in 2006, it appeared to be somewhat different in shape from those photographed earlier. *(Author's Collection)*

The City, the name by which a group of labourers' cottages at Harrow Weald was traditionally known (see also p. 124), had its very own public house, pictured here some time before the Second World War. Its first owners christened it The Case Is Altered, prompting still-active controversy as to the name's origins. *(Harrow Local History Collection)*

From its sign and other external decorations, the surviving inn seems to ignore the legal implications of its name in favour of a theory that the words are a corruption of the Spanish 'casa alta' or high house. The argument goes that this name was designed to win custom from local soldiers recently returned from the Peninsular Wars. *(Author's Collection)*

8

The Lanes That Were

Perhaps the most significant change of the last 100 years has been the
proliferation of traffic on important road-links that nevertheless still call
themselves 'lanes'. Oxhey Lane, which links Middlesex with Hertfordshire on
Stanmore's western fringe, is a case in point. Since this peaceful view was taken
in the early 1930s the 'lane' has been widened and modernised, losing the much-
loved boundary oak (centre), planted in 1823. *(Harrow Local History Collection)*

Oxhey Lane Farm, just yards from the county boundary, as it looked in 1911. At that time the lane still had a Coal Duty marker dating from the first years of the eighteenth century, when a tax was imposed on every ton of coal brought across the county border. *(Harrow Local History Collection)*

Though no longer a fully working establishment, Oxhey Lane Farm has happily survived with a beautifully restored farmhouse now adjoining a busy farm shop. Previous owners have included Henry John Smith, former proprietor of Harrow Weald's Red Lion (see p. 114), who died there in 1934 at the age of eighty-nine. *(Author's Collection)*

Providing a direct link between Greater and Lesser Stanmore (Whitchurch), Marsh Lane, pictured here some time in the 1930s, has always been one of the district's key thoroughfares. According to the *Victoria County History of Middlesex*, the boundary between the two parishes was so ill defined at this point that both sets of parishioners were allowed to graze their livestock there. *(Harrow Local History Collection)*

At the beginning of the twenty-first century, Marsh Lane happily retains a covering of trees along what is otherwise a ribbon-like development of flats and houses. At the Whitchurch Lane end it borders the so-called Stanmore Marsh, from which it takes its name. Once home to Stanmore's earliest gas company, the Marsh is now a small public open space. *(Author's Collection)*

A century ago the relatively few buildings that existed in Stanmore's lanes would have been picturesque homes such as Honeypot Lane's Marsh Cottages. Already in existence when the first official 1-inch Ordnance Survey Map appeared in 1807, they achieved a measure of fame in 1926 when they were featured in a film called *Huntingtower*, which starred the Scots music-hall comedian Sir Harry Lauder. Though listed, the cottages fell into such disrepair that demolition was permitted in about 1980. *(Author's Collection)*

Opposite, top: At least Green Lane is still reasonably green. A historic thoroughfare forming a triangle with Stanmore Hill and Church Road, it has also held on to many of its attractive small properties such as this nineteenth-century brick-built terrace known as Chart Cottages. This 1903 photograph seems to confirm local historian Roy Abbott's opinion that the street was nicknamed Jackdaw Lane because of 'the daily chattering over the garden gates'. *(Author's Collection)*

Opposite, bottom: Inevitably, 80 or so years later, the cottages have vehicles rather than people at their gates. Otherwise, Green Lane still lives up to the description given by historian Elizabeth Cooper in her 1983 *Strolls and Ambles* as a 'delightful road . . . with much variety of domestic buildings'. *(Author's Collection)*

The muddy state of Honeypot Lane in about 1925 lends credence to the widely accepted theory that its name was inspired by the perennial stickiness of its soil. Some sources, however, opt for a more sinister derivation, namely a corruption of *hangen-pytt* – or gibbet! *(Author's Collection)*

A fast, direct link between Stanmore and Queensbury/Kingsbury, Honeypot Lane is now as busy as any road in the Borough of Harrow and is lined on both sides with homes, shops and factories. It also has a public house called, inevitably, the Honeypot. Not surprisingly, its inn sign shows not a gibbet but a beehive! *(Author's Collection)*

Although it is now among the longest and busiest roads in the borough, extending all the way from Kenton Road through Belmont Circle to Uxbridge Road, Kenton Lane still makes a somewhat meandering progress that betrays the rural past seen in this pre-First World War photograph. The only house visible was then known as Hill House. *(Harrow Local History Collection)*

Same lane, same property, 90 years later. Now, however, it is so built up that the still-surviving property on the right carries a street number of 776! Much of this area once belonged to New College, Oxford, thanks to the generosity of a sixteenth-century graduate, Robert Sherborne, sometime Dean of St Paul's, who endowed it with some 190 acres of Harrow Weald land. *(Author's Collection)*

This view of Kenton Lane Farm in 1811 is taken from a book by the celebrated horticulturist John Claudius Loudon who had done pioneering work there. His prolific writings transformed Victorian taste in gardens, parks and farming practice. *(Author's Collection)*

Happily, Kenton Lane Farm is still in business, and its farmhouse remains. For more than half of the twentieth century it operated as Brazier's Dairy, whose milk floats were a familiar and welcome sight throughout the locality. Their advertising promised 'all milk from our own cows'. *(Author's Collection)*

9

Public Services

Stanmore's internationally renowned Royal National Orthopaedic Hospital has a
further claim to fame – a site on Brockley Hill that scholars now regard as the likeliest
location of Sulloniacae, the Roman staging post between London and Verulamium
(St Albans). In the belief that it was also the site of a battle between the Romans
under Julius Caesar and the British under Cassivellanus, a commemorative obelisk
was raised in 1750. Seen here in an undated but possibly 1930s photograph, it has
been largely swallowed up by sprawling hospital departments.
(Harrow Local History Collection)

Originally founded in London in 1838 – appropriately enough, by a man born with a club foot – what ultimately became the Royal National Orthopaedic Hospital opened its country branch at Brockley Hill, Stanmore, in July 1922. Not long afterwards these open-ended wards had been built to ensure ample fresh air for young tuberculosis patients. *(Author's Collection)*

This state-of-the-art swimming pool is just one part of the present Aspire Centre for patients with acute spinal injuries and, in turn, only one of 100-plus buildings on the 112-acre site. Recent press reports indicate that, if plans can be agreed, the whole hospital could undergo a £135 million rebuild in the foreseeable future. *(Author's Collection)*

Stanmore's tradition of hospital nursing goes right back to 1891 when a small cottage hospital was built in Old Church Lane at the expense of sisters Emily and Katherine Wickens, who lived at The Pynnacles. It cost some £2,000 and could receive eight patients for whom both an 'operating room' and a dispensary were provided. *(Harrow Local History Collection)*

Today, considerably extended, the building still stands. After some years as a geriatric hospital it was acquired in 1982 by the Jewish Society for the Mentally Handicapped, which later merged with the Ravenswood Foundation to run the Stanmore Cottage Residential Home for a small number of disabled adults. *(Author's Collection)*

In the early years of the last century, members of the Wealdstone and Stanmore Police Force
went to Stanmore to collect their weekly pay. On one such occasion, in 1907, the pay parade
provided the opportunity for a suitably serious group photograph. *(Harrow Local History
Collection)*

The present Stanmore Police Station at the Edgware end of Whitchurch Lane was built in
1932 on the site of an earlier Victorian station. When this picture was taken in spring 2006
its front office was 'temporarily closed' owing to recruitment problems unheard of in 1907.
(Author's Collection)

10

Common Land & Ponds

As street names such as Common Road, The Common and Little Common testify, much of the northern boundary of Stanmore and Harrow Weald remains common land, much to the delight of walkers, riders and artists. The Stanmore Common scene above could well be contemporary but a closer look at the central figures reveals the fashions of the early 1930s. *(Harrow Local History Collection)*

One of the so-called Spring Ponds at Little Common is seen here in an official picture taken for the old Greater London County Council in 1976. The ponds were created artificially, possibly as long ago as Saxon or Roman times; indeed, for centuries, the northernmost stretch of water was known as Caesar's Pond. *(Harrow Local History Collection)*

Thirty years later, the pond still presents an attractive appearance following a major effort by the local authority to rid its surface of an infestation of weeds. Posters now appeal to the public not to encourage the growth of algae by throwing excessive quantities of bread to the few remaining ducks. *(Author's Collection)*

Now that the Ponds form part of the official London Loop trail, the immediate surroundings have recently been made safer and more congenial for walkers through the provision of new wooden barriers, picnic tables and the occasional bench seat. *(Author's Collection)*

Little Common, pictured here about 50 years ago, almost certainly acquired its name when it was separated from the main expanse of Stanmore Common in 1637, at which time an acre was enclosed as a bowling green. The turreted mansion visible in the background is the original Stanmore Hall (see also p. 58). *(Harrow Local History Collection)*

Once a familiar local occasion but now unlikely ever to be repeated, the Berkshire Hunt is seen at its meet on Little Common some time in the 1930s. The choice of meeting place was possibly dictated by the fact that the Hunt's Master then lived in the immediate area. *(Author's Collection)*

The properties seen behind the hunters of 70 years ago still stand on Little Common which, for all the inevitable parked cars, retains much of its backwater charm. Many of the houses date from 1863 when Robert Hollond built stables and a laundry as well as a number of ornamental cottages. *(Author's Collection)*

11

St Lawrence & Whitchurch

St Lawrence, Whitchurch, is justly considered unique among Britain's parish
churches, not for its exterior which features this early sixteenth-century tower but for
its dramatic baroque interior (shown overleaf). The interior dates from the church's
rebuilding in about 1714 to the exacting standards of the man who was later to
become the mighty Duke of Chandos (see p. 93). Massively rich, he was able to
employ the great George Frederick Handel as his resident composer.
(Author's Collection)

This undated but presumably late nineteenth-century photograph delightfully recalls the time when Little Stanmore was largely rural – a time which almost certainly lasted until the third decade of the last century when the opening of Canons Park station in the self-same Whitchurch Lane brought in its wake the mixed benefits of suburbanisation. *(Harrow Local History Collection)*

A 2005 photograph from virtually the same viewpoint shows minimal change apart from an attractive lychgate dedicated in 1934 to the memory of Dr Alexander Findlater. An adjoining noticeboard reminds passers-by that Little Stanmore has traditionally been known as Whitchurch, supposedly because of the white-painted walls of the earliest church on this site. *(Author's Collection)*

The baroque beauty of the church's interior is fully captured in this 1930s photograph. Although building records are surprisingly limited, it is believed that the magnificent ceiling was the work of Louis Laguerre, with other painting done by the Venetian artist Antonio Bellucci. The Corinthian columns and other wood carving are definitely the work of the great Grinling Gibbons. *(Author's Collection)*

If anything, the interior is more beautiful than ever today following a two-phase restoration programme undertaken during the 1970s and '80s. Our picture shows the Mayor of Harrow and other dignitaries inspecting the work, which included the stripping of Victorian-applied varnish from all the church's woodwork, thus restoring its original golden oak colour. *(Author's Collection)*

The old Whitchurch Institute, formerly a National School, is shown here on Election Day, January 1906 (see also p. 33). The man in the car is the Hon. W.H. Peel, the Liberal Unionist candidate, who, in those almost carless days, found that an automobile was as good a way as any of attracting attention – and, hopefully, votes. *(Harrow Local History Collection)*

Opposite, top: It is surely somewhat ironic that a church so rich in genuine Handelian connections should perpetuate in its churchyard the myth that its one-time parish clerk and local blacksmith William Powell inspired Handel to write the famous composition known as *The Harmonious Blacksmith*. Whatever the inscription may say, the title was never used by Handel himself and was ascribed to the work only after the death of both men. *(Author's Collection)*

Opposite, bottom: For well over 250 years the so-called Lake Almshouses bordered the churchyard of St Lawrence. Originally endowed by Mary Lake, widow of Sir Thomas Lake, a distinguished servant of both Elizabeth I and James I, the houses were for the use of seven poor parishioners: four men and three women, all unmarried and regular in their church attendance.

Even at the start of the 1920s, Whitchurch Lane was quiet enough for sheep to be driven alongside the occasional cycle and pony and trap. According to local historian Alf Porter, the sheep were probably being herded to Angus Keen's farm which was located close to today's Handel Way. *(Author's Collection)*

The view of Whitchurch Lane near Handel Way is now the very antithesis of rural charm. A few older cottages, however, remain, their front rooms having been converted for a variety of commercial uses, ranging from chiropody to hairdressing. *(Author's Collection)*

12

Canons

Built in about 1712 for James Brydges, the 1st Duke of Chandos, the great house of Canons survived for little more than a quarter of a century. In its day, however, it was as grandiose a setting as any private individual had ever constructed, prompting admiration and derision in equal measure. This 1731 cartoon mocked its excesses, as did Alexander Pope in one of his best-known works. *(Author's Collection)*

Unable to find a single purchaser for house and grounds, the now debt-burdened family allowed the property to be broken up and sold piecemeal. At auction in 1747, the principal buyer was William Hallett, a London cabinetmaker, who replaced the original mansion with this much smaller house. *(Author's Collection)*

Hallett's house, which had salvaged much material from the original Canons, survives to this day. In 1929, it was purchased together with about 10 acres of land by the well-regarded North London Collegiate School, which added the classroom blocks shown here. *(Author's Collection)*

Among the very few actual survivors of the original Canons estate are this pair of ornamental gateposts, seen here in a photograph of 90 years ago. The gateposts are sited close to the junction of Edgware High Street and the road now known as Canons Drive. *(Author's Collection)*

Today the gate pillars are still in place, in large part thanks to the efforts of the Harrow Heritage Trust which, in 1998, found sufficient donors to ensure their refurbishment. Now an increasingly familiar and welcome sight throughout the borough, a nearby Heritage Trust 'brown plaque' commemorates the names of those responsible. *(Author's Collection)*

Perhaps even more surprising is the survival, also in Canons Drive, of this attractive water basin, once part of the ducal gardens. Families who come to observe the basin's wildlife are amused to find a sign – surely unique in a busy London borough – reading 'Slow – Ducks Crossing Road'. *(Author's Collection)*

Canons now gives its name to an extensive residential district (and local council ward) with its own Jubilee Line station in Whitchurch Lane. The station was to have been called Edgware (Whitchurch Lane) but this was changed in about 1932 to Canons Park, Edgware. A year later, it became simply Canons Park, the name in use today. *(Author's Collection)*

13

Belmont

As its earlier name of Bell Mount suggests, today's Belmont almost certainly
began life as an artificial feature created to provide visual interest within the
Canons estate (see p. 93). A touch of artificiality is also apparent in this picture
from about 1910 of local publican's daughter Marie Gunn (centre) and friends.
The adult Marie revealed that, in search of the picturesque, the photographer
had himself supplied the smocks and bonnets! *(Harrow Local History Collection)*

Some early confusion about the correct spelling of the district can be seen in this postcard view of 1906 which is identified as Belmount, Wealdstone. This time, however, the child's bonnet seems genuine enough. The signpost points the – not inconsiderable – way to Stanmore Golf Club. *(Harrow Local History Collection)*

By 1932 plans for extensive housing in the area had led to the building of a small, largely wooden railway station – in truth, little more than a halt – on the Stanmore–Harrow line originally opened (see p. 41) to bring guests to the hotel at Bentley Priory. As can be seen, Belmont Halt was then largely surrounded by fields. *(Harrow Local History Collection)*

Some five years later most of the fields had disappeared. In their place there were sufficient new homes to have justified the construction of a proper station, now known simply as Belmont, complete with centrally heated waiting room. When our picture was taken in the early 1950s steam trains were still in use. *(Harrow Local History Collection)*

In 1964 railway enthusiasts gathered at Belmont station to witness the very last train to run on the line which, it was claimed, had been losing money for years. It was, in fact, merely one of 2,128 stations recommended for closure in the highly unpopular Beeching Report. (*Harrow Local History Collection*)

Local cameramen were also quick to record the final stages of the demolition of Belmont station in 1966, two years after the axing of the line. By the time this particular picture was taken the only recognisable feature remaining was the first few steps of the station footbridge (top right). (*Author's Collection*)

After the removal of its tracks in 1968, a small part of the line at Belmont was opened as a nature trail and given the name of The Rattler, the nickname bestowed on the line's trains by generations of travellers. Little promoted or used, the trail was looking decidedly overgrown when our picture was taken in spring 2006. *(Author's Collection)*

Like so much of London's suburbia, Belmont developed rapidly in the 1930s and the presence of no fewer than three nearby housing estates was a primary factor in the construction not only of Belmont station but also the substantial shopping parade called Belmont Circle, seen here in a 1938 photograph. *(Harrow Local History Collection)*

Well over 60 years later, Belmont Circle has changed remarkably little except for the greater diversity of its shops, now clearly reflecting the area's multicultural population. Few of today's shoppers will be aware of early attempts to associate the name Belmont with Portia's great estate in Shakespeare's *The Merchant of Venice*. *(Author's Collection)*

14

Harrow Weald's Great Houses

It was a lucky day for Harrow when in autumn 1890 Sir William Gilbert first moved into the impressive mansion called Grim's Dyke at Old Redding, designed in 1870 by Richard Norman Shaw, whose own drawing of the entrance front is pictured here. Over a century later, the continued popularity of the comic operas Gilbert created with Sir Arthur Sullivan has ensured the house's survival as a hotel in an age when many similar mansions have had to be demolished. The name, incidentally, comes from an ancient defensive earthwork which runs through the grounds.

(Author's Collection)

Though its real fame dates from Gilbert's occupancy, Grim's Dyke was originally commissioned by the Royal Academician Frederick Goodall. He is shown here with one of the romantic Far Eastern paintings that made his fortune. Goodall later imported whole herds of Egyptian sheep and goats to Harrow Weald both to serve as models and to amuse his guests. *(Author's Collection)*

In this January 1904 drawing by a *Daily Mirror* artist, Gilbert is shown in his library at Grim's Dyke where once hung a Japanese executioner's sword said to have inspired arguably his most popular work, *The Mikado*. Trained as a barrister, Gilbert sat on the local magistrates' bench during his Harrow Weald years. *(Harrow Local History Collection)*

Waiters at the current Grim's Dyke Hotel are seen laying tables for tea in the beautiful gardens which Gilbert created during his 21 years in residence and which once required almost two dozen permanent staff. The hotel makes much of its Gilbertian connections, regularly offering both musical performances and guided tours. *(Author's Collection)*

This undated photograph shows the now-drained lake much as it looked in May 1911 when Sir William met his sudden and unexpected end. At seventy-four, he was swimming with two female guests when one of them got out of her depth. In attempting to save her, Sir William suffered a heart attack and died on the spot. *(Harrow Local History Collection)*

The Victorian taste for the neo-Gothic, as exemplified by the still-surviving Stanmore Hall (see p. 58), spilled over into neighbouring Harrow Weald when in 1870 Alexander Sim built this exuberantly decorated mansion, Harrow Weald Park, adjoining the junction of Uxbridge Road and Brookshill. An earlier house on the same site had been occupied by the Crockford family whose money came from the celebrated London gambling house of that name. *(Harrow Local History Collection)*

As lavishly appointed inside as out, Harrow Weald Park won the admiration of the local paper, the *Harrow Gazette*, which considered 'Harrow Weald particularly suitable for gentlemen's seats'. Few, however, could maintain such grandeur and the house was demolished in 1956 after the collapse of plans to turn it into a film studio. *(Author's Collection)*

Though the name Harrow Weald Park has survived, it now identifies a small estate reached by a private gated road. In 1990, perhaps conscious of their inheritance, 104 of its residents petitioned Harrow Council with a view to acquiring Conservation Area status; however, they failed to meet 'the criteria for formal designation'. *(Author's Collection)*

Several reminders of Harrow Weald Park's glory days survive following the conversion of many of its outbuildings, most notably the one-time North Lodge on Brookshill. In recent times, however, its charms have been somewhat overshadowed by an adjoining block of apartments. *(Author's Collection)*

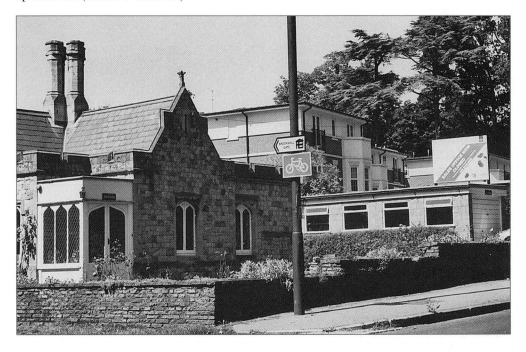

The Kiln which still survives in Common Road had this old kiln in its grounds, recalling the days when brick-making was a substantial local industry. From 1795, for almost a century, the property was in the hands of the entrepreneurial Blackwell family, who later founded the well-known Crosse & Blackwell business. A further reminder of local brick-making comes in the name of nearby Clamp Hill, a clamp being the term for a pile of bricks waiting to be fired. *(Harrow Local History Collection)*

During his Grim's Dyke residency, Frederick Goodall painted this attractive view of The Kiln, which shows the house to the left, the kiln in the middle and outbuildings to the right. The horse in the foreground had supposedly seen long service at Crosse & Blackwell's London premises: hence the title, *The Day of Rest in the Old Home. (Author's Collection)*

Virtually the same view is shown in this picture from the mid-1930s, which first appeared as an illustration in a 1938 book by Walter Druett called *Stanmore and Harrow Weald through the Ages*. Like the present author, Druett worked for the local paper before producing several works of local history. *(Author's Collection)*

Though the original Grade II Listed house still survives, for some few decades much of the estate has housed a popular gardening business. Originally known as The Kiln Garden Centre, it has recently been extensively rebuilt and currently trades under the name of Gardens Etc. (*Author's Collection*)

15

A Harrow Weald Miscellany

Given that the original parish of the now 912-year-old St Mary's, Harrow on the Hill, once stretched all the way from today's Wembley to Harrow Weald, it was inevitable that smaller churches would arise to meet the needs of people living far from the mother church. One of the first in 1815 was a small chapel in Uxbridge Road which, some three decades later, was rebuilt nearby as Harrow Weald's first parish church. With substantial additions, this is the present All Saints. *(Author's Collection)*

Although undated this engraving of All Saints was undoubtedly produced before 1890 as it still shows the original porch and bellcote. These were replaced by the present tower (see p. 111) designed by the noted Victorian architect William Butterfield who, as an old man, was asked to work on a number of further alterations, completed almost entirely at the expense of local philanthropist Thomas Blackwell. *(Harrow Local History Collection)*

As this recent picture taken from near the lychgate reveals, the approach to All Saints still has the look and feel of a country churchyard. This is in no small part due to the Nature Conservancy Council which, as part of their 'Living Churchyards' campaign, helps maintain it as a wildlife refuge. *(Author's Collection)*

In a second churchyard just across the road from the church lies the still-tended grave of William Leefe Robinson who won a Victoria Cross – and national fame – as the first airman in the First World War to bring down a German Zeppelin over British soil. Subsequently shot down himself and imprisoned, he was so weak on his return home that he quickly fell victim to the influenza epidemic of 1918. *(Author's Collection)*

Whereas comparable heroes of the First World War are now forgotten, Leefe Robinson's name lives on in this modern public house. It stands in the Uxbridge Road only yards from his last resting place and little more than a mile or so from his wartime lodgings in Gordon Avenue, Stanmore. *(Author's Collection)*

When photographed early last century, the public house (far right) at the junction of High Road and College Road, Harrow Weald, was called the Red Lion, like its predecessors on this corner since 1741. Embedded in the pavement outside was an old sarsen stone discovered by licensee William Smith in 1838. *(Author's Collection)*

In more recent times, the sarsen stone has been identified as the original Weald Stone, mentioned in the Court Rolls of both Henry VII and Henry VIII. A Harrow Heritage Plaque now mounted outside the pub also recalls that the stone gave its name to the adjoining district of Wealdstone, which had previously been known as Station End. *(Author's Collection)*

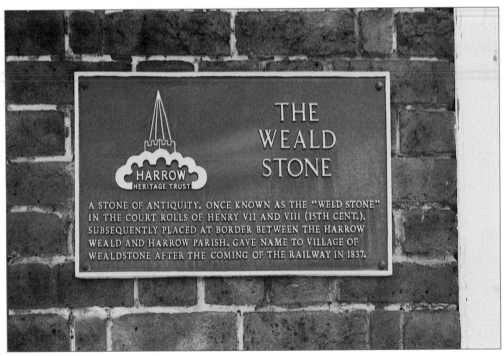

Today the Weald Stone is clearly displayed on the forecourt outside the public house which has been renamed the Weald Stone Inn. It is presumed that the stone once served as a boundary marker between the area then known as The Weald and the parish of Harrow on the Hill. *(Author's Collection)*

In 2006 the junction of College Road and High Road still retains some of the original buildings seen in the picture on the opposite page. College Road, like other 'college' names in the area, recalls the College of St Andrew's, a short-lived educational venture on the part of the Revd Edward Munro, first vicar of Harrow Weald. *(Author's Collection)*

Angered that so much of Harrow Weald's common land had been taken away from the people by the early nineteenth-century Enclosure Acts, local landowner Thomas Blackwell, one-time chairman of Crosse & Blackwell, attempted to 'adjust the balance' by giving 15 acres to the village in 1895 for use as a recreation ground. *(Author's Collection)*

On Thomas Blackwell's death in 1907, the ordinary folk of Harrow Weald repaid his generosity by building in his memory a charming and typically Edwardian entrance to the ground, which is still in use today. Alongside it the parish subsequently built its 1914–18 Roll of Honour. Among its three dozen listings there are three Blackwells. *(Author's Collection)*

Right from the outset, Blackwell's gift was not merely welcomed by the community but fully used. Here, for example, is the All Saints' Football Club at the ground, *c.* 1905. The older gentleman with hat and cane (centre) is the vicar, the Revd W.H. Peers, well liked as a keen supporter and occasional referee. *(Harrow Local History Collection)*

The Common, though vastly reduced from its original 1,500 acres, remains Harrow Weald's other great open space. The picture, which could well be contemporary, was in fact especially taken for Walter Druett's 1938 local history publication, *Stanmore and Harrow Weald through the Ages*. *(Harrow Local History Collection)*

Captured some time in the 1950s, this view looking up Harrow Weald's High Road towards Uxbridge Road shows a largely empty street with, on the left, the Edwardian gateway to the recreation ground and, on the right, the Harrow Weald Memorial Club. This substantial and popular venue was built in 1921 at a cost of only £6,000. *(Author's Collection)*

In today's High Road the Memorial Club has a relatively new neighbour in a Drive-Thru branch of the KFC fast-food franchise. It replaces the pleasant old property that for a time housed the Harrow Arts Centre. The latter subsequently found a new home at the Elliott Hall, Hatch End. *(Author's Collection)*

For many decades the site of today's Fontwell Close, just off the High Road/Uxbridge Road junction, was best known for the army transit camp established there within days of the outbreak of the First World War in 1914. No pictures seem to have survived of the camp but we do have this poignant reminder of the Seaforth Highlanders marching through nearby Wealdstone High Street. They are undoubtedly en route to the camp – and to a likely death in the trenches. *(Author's Collection)*

Today Fontwell Close is a peaceful residential backwater that bears no trace of its dramatic past. Its residents would probably be surprised to learn that the men who once camped there included a very young Warwickshire Regiment lieutenant destined to achieve fame in a later war as Field Marshal Bernard Montgomery. *(Author's Collection)*

Harrow Weald's agricultural past is vividly evoked by this early twentieth-century photograph of shepherd, flock and dog in the yard of the farm that then existed on the north side of the Weald Lane/High Road junction. At the time it was known as Weald Farm but, like so many other farms, its name not infrequently changed to reflect a new ownership. *(Author's Collection)*

By the time of this later view of the same corner, the property was known as Durrant's Farm. Although the picture's detail is admittedly far from clear, it remains of interest in that it shows a milk roundsman's horse stopping for a drink at the farm pond which was then a familiar feature of the local scene. *(Author's Collection)*

Over the years a wholly unproven theory has been mooted to the effect that Durrant's was the 'tumbledown' farm to which the novelist Anthony Trollope moved as a schoolboy when financial troubles forced his family to leave their grand Harrow Hill home. Perhaps for this reason the name is currently recalled in the apartment block Durrant Court on the Wealdstone side of the High Road. *(Author's Collection)*

With its proliferation of street furniture and numerous shops including a Waitrose superstore (middle distance, right), today's Weald Lane/High Road junction could hardly be more different from its Victorian counterpart. The one substantial link with the past is now the Weald Stone, just out of picture on the right. *(Author's Collection)*

For the better part of four centuries, Weald Lane was also the setting for the handsome Wealdstone House. Almost certainly beginning life as a farm, the property had long connections with the farming Dancer family although, by the nineteenth century, their increased prosperity caused them to be classified as 'gentry'. The house was demolished in September 1947. (*Harrow Local History Collection*)

The best known of the family, the nineteenth-century Daniel Dancer, achieved considerable notoriety as a miser and may well have been the model for Charles Dickens's Scrooge. When he died in 1794, a search of his run-down Astmiss Farm revealed several hidden hoards, including £2,500 concealed in a dung heap. (*Author's Collection*)

Another member of the philanthropic Blackwell family, Charles Blackwell, was responsible for building a number of workers' cottages in the street called Old Redding, one of which is seen here in an early 1930s picture. The cottages, among the first of their kind in the country, originally housed about thirty labourers engaged in the family's farming and brick-making businesses. *(Harrow Local History Collection)*

Blackwell's little 'estate', shown here in an attractive between-wars winter study, subsequently took on the gloriously incongruous name of The City. Some sources even suggest that its pub, The Case Is Altered (see also p. 70), was widely known as The City's 'Cathedral'! (*Author's Collection*)

Today The City has vanished apart from its pump, whose protective canopy can be glimpsed both in the picture on p. 123 and the one above. The origin of the present name Old Redding is unclear but may well stem from Old Rydding, identified in a manorial survey of 1547 as a field belonging to Pinner's Woodhall Farm. (*Author's Collection*)

16

Edgware

The otherwise separate community of Edgware owes its brief inclusion in this book to the fact that the Little Stanmore side of its High Street lies in the Borough of Harrow. The High Street is, in fact, part of the great Roman road known as Watling Street which ran from Dover to Chester via London and St Albans. Its characteristic Roman straightness is clearly visible in this 1880s view, when coaching inns prospered on both sides of the road. *(Author's Collection)*

One of the most popular of the nine hostelries on the Little Stanmore side was the Chandos Arms, a rambling timber-framed building dating from at least the sixteenth century. Once the Crane, it had been renamed in honour of the Duke of Chandos (see p. 93). Its neighbour was the old Edgware Courthouse where Sir William Gilbert of Grim's Dyke occasionally sat as a magistrate and which remained in use until 1913. *(Author's Collection)*

Once owned by the Stanmore brewer Thomas Clutterbuck, the Chandos Arms was also the home of the Edgware Fire brigade who maintained their fire-engine station in the stableyard at the rear of the inn. The brigade, pictured here in about 1900, also served the Stanmores which were lucky enough to have an ample reserve of natural water (see p. 83). *(Harrow Local History Collection)*

Much of the impetus for change in Edgware stemmed from the ambitions of the London Underground network which, in August 1924, opened a station on the site of a barn in what was still essentially a country road. By 1931, the date of this picture, present-day Edgware had already begun to take shape all around it. *(Harrow Local History Collection)*

Almost three-quarters of a century later, the immediate vicinity of Edgware station is just about recognisable although the small local businesses have long since been swallowed up by the sizeable Broadwalk shopping mall. Since the station also doubles as a bus terminus, pedestrians must now negotiate that near-constant flow of traffic which has become one of the most dominant features of contemporary life in Stanmore and Edgware alike. *(Author's Collection)*

ACKNOWLEDGEMENTS

This, my ninth book, is rather special to me in several ways. First, it completes a trilogy of Past & Present titles for Sutton Publishing, the others being *Harrow* (2001) and *Pinner* (2002). Even more importantly, it enables me to match – in output if not in achievement – the career of a distinguished predecessor, Walter Druett, who also moved into local history after years of editorial writing for the *Harrow Observer*. Over 60 years ago he produced, in succession, a Harrow . . . a Pinner . . . and a Stanmore book in a series called *Through the Ages*, all of which are still readily available, and hugely enjoyable.

Finally, this book has helped strengthen my long-time collaboration with Harrow's Local History Librarian Bob Thomson who, on this occasion, has not only loaned me many valuable pictures from the borough's Local History Collection but has also ensured that my captions are both accurate and lucid.

May I also express my heartfelt thanks to the many other writers who have similarly found inspiration in the history of Stanmore, including Bob Thomson himself, Alfred E. Porter, Alan W. Ball, Peter G. Scott and especially Eileen Bowlt. The latter's *Stanmore Past* (1998) is surely essential reading for anyone in search of a more detailed and scholarly history.